ART DECO
SCULPTURE

ART DECO SCULPTURE

CHRYSELEPHANTINE STATUETTES OF THE TWENTIES AND THIRTIES

VICTOR ARWAS

ACADEMY EDITIONS·LONDON / ST. MARTIN'S PRESS·NEW YORK

Sources and Acknowledgements
There is very little source material available on chryselephantine figures of the 1920s and 1930s. The Ideal Home Exhibition Catalogues mention Preiss with reference to the Phillips and MacConnal Stand, and Phillips and MacConnal themselves brought out a slim brochure which illustrates a very few Preiss figures, each illustrated model being numbered, and I should like to express grateful thanks to Mr. Richard Feiner of New York for allowing me access to his copy which has the original prices added by hand. The annual Catalogues of the Salons are helpful, as are the regular fully illustrated Etling Catalogues. There is also a separate Chiparus brochure from Etling.

Recent research by Reto Niggl in Antiquitäten-Zeitung and the catalogues of the Ivory Museum in Erbach have also been very useful.

All photographs unless otherwise credited were provided by Editions Graphiques Gallery, London.

Back cover

PIERRE LE FAGUAYS *Salome* cold-painted bronze and carved ivory on marble base

Published in Great Britain by
Academy Editions 7 Holland Street London W8

Published in the U.S.A. in 1975 by St Martin's Press Inc.
175 Fifth Avenue New York NY 10010

Library of Congress Catalog Card Number 74-29068
ISBN 0-312-05251-0 (U.S.A. only)

Printed and bound in Shen Zhen, China.

The sculptural qualities of ivory have always attracted artists and craftsmen. Soft enough to carve with ease, compact enough to allow the most delicate and intricate of patterns, ivory has a brilliant sheen when polished. It can remain a dazzling white for centuries, although exposure to dust and sunlight may yellow it attractively. Prehistoric carvings of parts of mammoth tusks have been found; Chinese-carved ivory figures have long been collected; the Japanese have turned tusks into tall immortals and tiny netsuke. In the Middle Ages in Europe ivory was used to glorify God and adorn the fair. Hollowed sections were turned into elaborate steins, vases, and cornucopias. The rot had set in. By the middle of the nineteenth century, ivory in Europe was being used almost exclusively for the production of such art objects as the backs of brushes, door handles and shoe horns. The elephant tusks reaching China and Japan came mostly from India, although African tusks were generally longer and of better quality.

With the conquest of the Congo, the situation changed. Exploited ruthlessly and cruelly, the Congo yielded to Europe blood-stained riches of precious wood and minerals. Public outcries at the cruelty and callousness of the administrators and overseers served no purpose, since the Congo was the personal property of the King of the Belgians. It took several years of international pressure to transfer the administration of the Congo Free State to the Belgian government whose approach was rather more humane. Ivory tusks from the Congo Free State were shipped to Belgium in enormous quantities which far exceeded the needs for their rather restricted uses. In 1894, the Secretary of State for the Congo Free State, Monsieur Van Estvelde, called on Belgian artists to use ivory as their medium. Artists willing to use ivory were intially offered elephant tusks free, and artists registered in order to choose their pieces. There was official encouragement in the form of commissions and exhibitions.

In 1894 the Antwerp International Exhibition established a new colonial section. This contained native artifacts—weapons, fabrics, ornaments—as well as the first art objects fashioned in ivory. These first works were exhibited and looked at 'rather as products of the Congo than *objets d'art*'

as Fernand Khnopff wrote in *The Studio*. The Cercle Artistique of Brussels, however, held a later separate exhibition of these same objects, and this time they had an enormous impact on the viewers. The possibilities of ivory appealed increasingly to artists, particularly to the Symbolist and art nouveau artists, whose rejection of 'official' art encouraged them to look at new materials.

In 1897, the colonial section of the Brussels Exhibition, held at the Tervueren Palace, had a separate chryselephantine section. The term chryselephantine was originally used to describe statues made of gold and ivory in classical Greece. The Belgians extended the meaning to encompass an object fashioned in ivory in combination with any other material, such as bronze, onyx, marble, or wood. At the Brussels Exhibition carved ivory statuettes vied with mysterious, hieratic objects of metal and ivory, often encrusted with precious stones. Philippe Wolfers exhibited vases with bronze swans, their necks entwined round an ivory pillar. Khnopff himself showed a sightless mask of tinted ivory and partly enamelled bronze. Egide Rombaud exhibited an ivory group, though his greatest success was at the Paris 1900 Exhibition, where he showed candelabra consisting of ivory nymphs amid wrought silver plants by Franz Hoosemans. Flesh coloured marble nudes exhibited in Paris by Jean-Léon Gérome startled and then horrified critics, to whom applied colour was anathema, and concealed, they felt, both the ability of the sculptor and the honesty of the material used. Other artists were not slow to see the possibilities inherent in multimedia and polychrome sculpture. Jean Dampt created a superb composition of a silvery knight in full armour embracing a jewelled ivory maiden; Ernest Barrias made several versions in different materials of his *Nature unveiling herself before Science*; Théodore Rivière made a bronze and ivory version of his *Carthage*, a scene from the play inspired by Gustave Flaubert's novel, in which Mathô embraces the feet of Salammbô, played by Sarah Bernhardt. The critics screamed louder still: these romantic confections were an outrage and a failure, imitations of life which betrayed their artificiality because unlike Pygmalion's creation they did not come to life. They were not sculpture, they were mere *objets d'art*. This did not really disturb

FERNAND KHNOPFF *Mask* tinted ivory, bronze and enamel (The Studio)

EGIDE ROMBAUX *Nymph Candelabra* wrought silver and ivory, quartz base 16.5 in; 42 cm. The silver was designed by Franz Hoosemans for C. G. Hallberg of Stockholm

established artists who were, in fact, engaged in the production of romantic confections such as Clovis Delacour's *Andromeda*, a tall ivory nude with turquoises in her hair, chained to a granite rock within a turbulent sea of carved onyx from which a fearsome bronze dragon emerges. The revelation that ancient Egyptian and classical Hellenic sculpture was normally tinted and coloured enabled the sculptors to cock a snook at the critics, and to point out in lofty tones that the *Athena Parthenos* by Phydias was chryselephantine.

The International Exhibition of 1900 in Paris showed several chryselephantine sculptures, mostly Symbolist, and several were shown at the Royal Academy in London, the Libre Esthétique Salon in Brussels, and the Secession Exhibitions in Vienna and Munich. In England Sir George Frampton exhibited his *Lamia*, a large bust made of bronze and ivory, and studded with opals, which was inspired by Keats's poem; and Sir Alfred Gilbert exhibited an aluminium and ivory statuette of *St. George and the Dragon* at the Royal Academy in 1896, before it was placed on the royal pew in Sandringham Church. Multimedia sculpture was precious in conception and execution, a curiosity to be attempted occasionally rather than the norm.

Experimental sculptors tended increasingly towards simplicity of material and technique, the artistic conception being of greater importance than the display of skill in the use of diverse materials. The outbreak of war in 1914 inevitably interrupted the even tenor of the salons. By 1918, the whole artistic avant-garde had shifted. Many of the pre-war innovators were dead; dada, cubism and futurism were shifting the future direction of mainstream sculpture. The salons, although diminished in number and influence, still had the power of patronage, and public statuary persisted in its search for 'classicism'. The critical jibes against multimedia figures meant that the normal salons were not open to them. The growing interest in furniture and interior design had inspired a new annual exhibition, the Salon des Artistes Décorateurs. This salon, the Salon des Artistes Français, and the Salon des Indépendants were to be the home of much of the new generation of multimedia figures.

The application of modern techniques to these creations meant that they need no longer be exclusively reserved for the very rich. The bronze, or other metal, could be cast quickly and at reasonable expense. Variety could be achieved by

E. BARRIAS *Nature unveiling herself before Science* silver and silver gilt and ivory, lapis lazuli base 25 in; 63.5 cm

THEODORE RIVIERE *Carthage* Sarah Bernhardt in the role of Salammbô. Gilt bronze and ivory, verde marble base 15.25 in; 44.4 cm. First exhibited at the Dresden Exhibition 1901

either traditional application of patina or by cold-painting the metal. The ivory, of course, had to be carved by hand, but this was simplified somewhat by providing minutely measured models which could be carved by craftsmen to the artist's approval. The result is that no two figures could be carved identically; there are always differences of expression. The ivory was often tinted or coloured, the hair dyed, and the eyes, lips and cheeks made up.

The figurine artists who emerged in the years after the First World War fall broadly into four streams, hieratic, naturalistic, erotic, and stylised, although obviously all have some degree of stylisation, and some artists worked in more than one style.

The hieratic artists are very close to the artists of the 1890s. Their creations are often mysterious queens of the night, dancers wrapped in the metallic folds of rare and costly fabrics and encrusted with jewels at wrist and ankle, their movements frozen into strange theatrical attitudes. They reflect the two new great art forms that were exciting Paris and the world: the Ballets Russes and the cinema. The Ballets Russes had been stranded in Paris because of the war and the Russian revolution of 1917. Organised by Diaghilev

to show off the most original Russian dancers, choreographers, composers and designers, their impact on art and decoration was enormous. The impact of the cinema was greater still. Millions of people throughout the world were lost in the celluloid dream, passionately loving their favourite stars, aping their mannerisms, dress and hairstyles. It was a pure, visual and narrative art, unencumbered with sound. The actors evolved a stylised code of communication in which gesture replaced words, and the gesture was extravagant and larger than life: grief, joy, love, fear and hate existed, and were seen to exist. Some directors responded within the technical limitations of lighting and camera mobility, creating the mechanistic extravagance of *Metropolis*, or the haunting terrors of German expressionist films.

The two most interesting 'hieratic' figurine artists are Colinet and Chiparus. Claire Jeanne Roberte Colinet was born in Brussels, where she studied sculpture with Jef Lambeaux. She moved to Paris, where she was elected to membership of the Société des Artistes Français, and exhibited at the Salon from 1913, gaining an Honourable Mention in 1914. She exhibited at the Salon des Indépendants from 1937 to 1940. Her best figures

CHIPARUS *Danseuse de Kapurthala* patinated bronze and carved ivory on onyx base 21.75 in; 55 cm

CHIPARUS *Clair de Lune* patinated bronze and ivory on onyx base 23 in; 58 cm

display a powerful sense of composition in space, the limbs and hands arranged in strange balletic poses. Dimitri Chiparus, a Rumanian, came to Paris to study under A. Mercié and J. Boucher, and later Gallicised his forename to Démetre. He exhibited at the Salon des Artistes Français from 1914, when he received an Honourable Mention, to 1928. His figures include small-scale, realistic representations of nudes and women in everyday clothes, a number of Pierrots and Columbines, and theatrical dancers which were almost certainly based on actual performers. They strut, pirouette, kick; the line from arm to arm to spine to leg curves alarmingly. Others stand on tiptoe, arms turned above the head or balanced on ethereal rests. Some are right out of the Ballets Russes, others from a smoky Parisian nightclub. And some are heroines from a serial by Feuillade, the true vampire-women, cloaked and cuirassed, the promise of the abyss. Henry Fugère can also be included in this stream. Born at Saint Mandé in 1872, he studied with Cavelier, Barrias and M. D. Puech, and exhibited at the Salon des Artistes Français, where he was awarded an Honourable Mention in 1927.

The most important of the 'naturalistic' stream was F. Preiss. Johann Philippe Ferdinand Preiss was born in 1882 in the ivory-carving town of Erbach in the Odenwald in Germany. Two years of apprenticeship were followed by several more as an ivory carver in Milan and Baden-Baden. In 1906 he joined with a fellow carver, Arthur Kassler, to found a firm of ivory turners and carvers in Berlin called Preiss & Kassler. Preiss married in 1907 and, three years later, they shortened the name of the firm to PK. They were joined by a bronze founder and two more ivory carvers and expanded the business to specialise in multimedia figures, mostly inspired by classical sculpture. The PK firm closed down in 1914 at the outbreak of war, reopening in 1919, and soon

Plate I
CHIPARUS *Danseuse* patinated and silvered-bronze, tinted ivory, on stepped marble base 52 cm (Editions Graphiques Gallery, London. Photo: Rodney Todd-White)

Plate II
F. PREISS *Flame Leaper* cold-painted bronze, tinted ivory and composition flames on stepped black marble base 34 cm (Editions Graphiques Gallery, London. Photo: Rodney Todd-White)

Plate III
F. PREISS *Autumn Dancer* cold-painted bronze and tinted ivory on green onyx and black marble base 38 cm (Author's collection)

IV

VI

VIII

employed ten sculptors. Preiss himself designed most models, often using photographs of real dancers and sporting figures. The actual carving of the ivory is invariably exquisite, the faces sweet and pretty, the hands and fingers slender and graceful. The bronze is usually cold-painted in cool colours, silver, blue and grey; warm colours were used very sparingly. A particular photograph was sometimes used as the subject for interpretation by more than one artist of the firm. Thus almost identical subjects are found with different signatures. Another famous German workshop was the firm of Rosenthal and Maeder whose artists included Prof. O. Poerzl, Philippe and Harders. All their sculptures were usually marked with the firm's RuM monogram until 1929 when they were taken over by Preiss' PK firm. PK and RuM figures were distributed in Great Britain by the Phillips and MacConnal Gallery of Arts which published a loose-leaf catalogue illustrating them and giving model numbers, with particular emphasis on the work of Preiss himself.

Preiss produced a number of figures of children, some nude, some clothed, some dressed up in nineteenth century adult-style clothes; the pre-war classical nudes gave way to the post-war 'modern' nudes, lithe, athletic, elegant in movement; a few dancers, inspired by stars of the cinema and music-hall — Brigitte Helm as the human heroine of *Metropolis*, the *Bat Dancer* from the Fred Astaire and Ginger Rogers movie *Going Down to Rio*, Ada May, a C.B. Cochran revue dancer in *Lighter Than Air*; and there are the Olympians.

The Olympic figures are a perfect representation of the worship of physical beauty and sport which

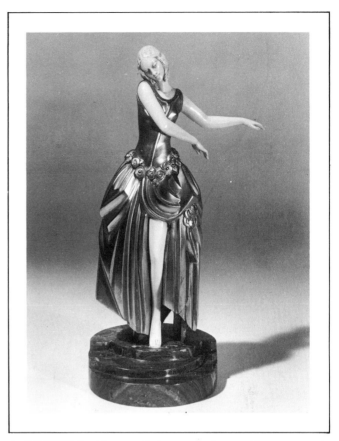

A. GUERVAL *Le Menuet* gilt bronze and carved ivory on verde marble base 10.25 in; 26 cm

F. PREISS *The Tennis Player* cold-painted bronze and carved ivory on banded onyx base 11.25 in; 29 cm

Plate IV
GERDAGO *Carnaval* enamelled bronze and carved ivory on onyx base

Plate V
GERDAGO *Charleston Dancer* enamelled bronze and carved ivory on onyx base

Plate VI
GERDAGO *Temple Dancer* polished and enamelled bronze and tinted ivory on green onyx base 47 cm (Collection Elton John, Windsor. Photo: Rodney Todd-White)

Plate VII
GERDAGO *Exotic Dancer* gilt and enamelled bronze and tinted ivory on green onyx base 36 cm (Collection Elton John, Windsor. Photo: Rodney Todd-White)

Plate VIII
A. KELETY *Les Coeurs* etched and silver-inlaid bronze and tinted ivory on marble base (Author's Collection)

had spread from Soviet Russia in the twenties and had led to parades and alarming outdoor displays of physical prowess and rhythmic ensemble movements in London, Paris and Rome, until its sponsorship by Hitler in the thirties and forties came to equate it forever with the mindless marches of Fascism. Preiss's Olympic pantheon includes male and female tennis players and golfers, a boy skier, and girls playing golf, throwing a javelin, bathing, ice skating, and sprinting. Vibrantly alive, they echo Leni Riefenstahl's cinematic hymn to physical movement at the Berlin Olympics.

K. Lorenzl, who also designed ceramics for the Austrian firm of Goldscheider, often copied well-known Preiss figures, such as the *Con Brio*, though he was not as good a carver. At his best, however, Lorenzl depicted with affection and admiration, the new woman, slender and boyish in shape, hair bobbed or *à la garçonne*, dressed in fashionably floppy pyjamas or as an Amazon. Some of his figures are signed K. Lor and Ronr. Jean Descomps, born at Agen, was a member of the Société des Artistes Français and exhibited at their salons, gaining an Honourable Mention in 1901, and a Third Class Medal in 1903. He also designed several bas-relief plaques and figures in pâte-de-verre for the firm of Almeric Walter at Nancy.

The 'erotic' category embraces far fewer artists. Charol, whose smouldering girl wears one green stocking and one long green glove to match the colour of her hair, is illustrated, as are works by Bruno Zach. Zach is the depictor of the perverse, creating kinky, highly sophisticated women dressed in leather trouser suits, insolently smoking cigarettes; swirling-skirted girls fighting the wind; girls in slips or gartered stockings holding whips; dancers doing a high kick; and haughty girls naked beneath their parted fur coats. They are the dream mistresses of sado-masochistic Berlin between the wars. Although most of Zach's figures are in bronze, his rare chryselephantine figures are especially worth collecting.

The last of the streams is the 'stylised'. This convenient word gathers in a host of influences which came to reflect the 1920s and 1930s: a little of the Ballets Russes; the angularities of the Glasgow style and the Bauhaus; the popularisation of cubism (which according to Jean Cocteau became a smart catchword for anything modern and peculiar); the experiment into simplification of form by Brancusi and Nadelmann; the visual

CHIPARUS *Orilla* patinated bronze and carved ivory on onyx base 24.5 in; 62 cm

excitement of simultaneity by Robert and Sonia Delaunay. Features are simplified and stylised, and the treatment of clothing is increasingly geometric and decorative, without any attempt at realism. The artists here include Le Faguays, Philippe, Kelety, Roland Paris, and Sarabezolles.

Pierre Le Faguays was born at Nantes. He was elected a member of the Société des Artistes Français and exhibited at their salons, gaining an Honourable Mention in 1926. He was also a member of the La Stèle and Evolution groups in which artist craftsmen exhibited bronzes, ceramics, lamps and other decorative objects. Alexander Kelety was born in Budapest, Hungary, and studied sculpture with Imre Simay before going to France, where he exhibited at the Salon des Artistes Français. Charles (known as Carlo) Sarabezolles was born in Toulouse. A student under Mercié and Marqueste, he was elected to the Société des Artistes Français and exhibited at the salons, where he was awarded an Honourable Mention in 1912, a Silver Medal in 1921, and the National Prize in 1922. The monumental version of his *L'Ame de la France* was purchased by the State. Philippe, an Austrian artist, created stylish

CHIPARUS *Miro* patinated bronze and carved ivory on onyx base 22.5 in; 57 cm

models and dancers whose gestures are theatrical and enormously effective. His treatment of the clothes in *The Swirling Dress* is a pure product of the new Machine Age. Gerdago figures are strongly geometric, the folds of the clothes angular, the bronze cold-painted with brilliant enamel colours.

Roland Paris employs a completely different stylisation. Born in Vienna in 1894, he studied under Henry Van der Velde, the architect and designer who was one of the founders of the Bauhaus School. He is caricatural and satirical, influenced by the savage humour of George Grosz or Otto Dix. His figures are often savagely funny, mock-crudely executed, absurdly extravagant.

Of course there were many other artists creating chryselephantine figures in the 1920s and 1930s, including Marcel Bouraine, Lamourdedieu, Alonzo, Gallo, Gilbert, Godard, Sosson, Hoffman. And many figures are unsigned and unattributed.

The bases of art deco chryselephantine figures are often an important part of the composition. The 1890s had shown that lapis lazuli and veined marble in the base enhanced the status of the statuette as a precious art object. In the twenties and thirties onyx, seamed and veined, polished and glowing, became the preferred material, along with marble. The most elaborate bases were devised by Chiparus: stepped pyramids, multiple sided and decorated with mosaics or with inset bronze plaques. Preiss also used a variety of bases, although they are much less elaborate, and are usually green onyx or black marble with gold veining. More elaborate bases have banded layers of green onyx and black marble. Most, but by no means all, of the figures are signed. The signatures are sometimes on the figures, but are most often found on the base. Collectors should beware of trusting exclusively to signatures, since a spurious figure can easily be placed on a signed base, just as some very fine figures may not be signed. When a model is known, and the quality and state of preservation are good, a signature is unimportant. Bases also sometimes have the mark of the bronze founder or of the firm commissioning the figure, such as the PK (Preiss & Kassler) or RuM (Rosenthal und Maeder) marks. Some figures by Kelety and Lorenzl have the Goldscheider mark; and several figures by Chiparus and Colinet were cast and exhibited by Etling.

The chryselephantine figures of the nineties were expensive *objets d'art* for aesthetes and dandies. Those of the twenties and thirties were designed to appeal to the bourgeoisie as decorative objects suitable as presentation gifts for weddings and retirements, although varied enough to appeal to the collector's instinct. A brochure produced by Phillips and MacConnal gives detailed instructions for the construction of suitable niches for the display of Preiss figures. Interestingly enough, although they may be found in every country in the world, each country had its preferred artists. Preiss and Lorenzl figures are found primarily in Great Britain and the United States, Colinet, Philippe, Bouraine and Le Faguays in France, and Roland Paris and Bruno Zach primarily in Germany. Chiparus figures are found in France, Great Britain and the United States, but his large figures turn up in a number of palaces in India, where they obviously appealed to the extravagant tastes of the Maharajahs who collected art objects and Rolls Royces by the ship's holdful. The success of bronze and ivory figurines brought about a host of cheap imitations, usually fashioned very crudely of heavily decorated soft metal with faces, limbs, and hands moulded in 'ivorine', a plastic composition made and coloured to resemble

EMILIO VILLANIS *Dalila* Cabinet figure. Gilt bronze and ivory, pink veined marble base 8.5 in; 21.6 cm

GODARD *Danseuse Hindoue* patinated and silver-inlaid bronze and ivory on marble base 51.5 cm (Editions Graphiques Gallery, London)

ivory and sometimes containing powdered ivory to give it more substance. These sad, mass-produced lumps are often confused with, and even touted as, bronze and ivory figures, and were the main reason why the figures fell into such disrepute. Chryselephantine figures were not considered as works of art but as decoration by the critics of their day, who tended to suffer from the debilitating disease of 'good taste'. When it became smart to collect art deco, it was ceramics, glass, furniture, silver, jewellery and sculpture that was sought, while bronze and ivory figures were still rejected. For several years the two main London auction houses refused to include these figures in their specialised sales. The situation has now changed significantly. New collectors have swelled the ranks, and every auction sale brings new record prices. In 1972 an important exhibition of these figures was held at Editions Graphiques Gallery, London, and later transferred to the Aberdeen Art Gallery and Museum, while the

B.B.C. televised a few minutes of figures whirling on turntables.

In an era when so many of the pompous claims of scribbler-seekers for this or that Great Work of Art have been deflated, the smaller scale merits of chryselephantine figures of the twenties and thirties have come into their own. They reflect and incorporate many of the artistic discoveries and preoccupations of the early part of the twentieth century as they were interpreted for the bourgeois sensitivities of the day, and as such are a precious link with their time. Unpretentious and certainly highly decorative, they have become accepted far more widely than at the time of their first inception.

Several major collections have been formed, and the final accolade of fame has been bestowed on them: modern fakes, made in France, England and the United States, are flooding the market. Seeing these fakes makes one's admiration for the exquisite originals grow even more.

THE ILLUSTRATIONS

CHIPARUS *Kora* patinated bronze and ivory
on stepped onyx base 24.5 in; 62 cm

CHIPARUS *The Hoop Girl* gilt bronze and ivory, brown onyx
base 10.25 in; 26 cm

CHIPARUS *Le Coup de Vent (Windblown)* gilt bronze and ivory,
onyx base 11 in; 27.9 cm

Opposite
CHIPARUS *Testris* cold-painted bronze and ivory, brown onyx
base 25.75 in; 63.5 cm

CHIPARUS *Genre Dancer* gilt bronze and ivory, black and gold marble base 18.6 in; 47.25 cm (Sotheby's)

Opposite

F. PREISS *Invocation* (Model No. 1083) cold-painted bronze and ivory, black and gold marble base 14 in; 36 cm. This first sold for 21 gns, with an all bronze version at 12 gns

CHIPARUS *Danseuse Nubienne* gilt bronze and ivory, stepped black and gold marble base with inset bronze panel 16.5 in; 42 cm

CHIPARUS *Male Cymbal Dancer* bronze and ivory, brown onyx base 16.5 in; 42 cm (Sotheby's)

CHIPARUS *The Long Skirt* gilt bronze and ivory, beige onyx base 7.5 in; 19 cm

CHIPARUS *Russian Dancer* gilt bronze and ivory, black and gold marble base with inset oval bronze panels 22 in; 56 cm

CHIPARUS *Pirouette* cold-painted bronze and ivory, veined
onyx base 18.5 in; 47 cm

CHIPARUS *Dancer* cold-painted bronze and ivory, brown
onyx base 15.5 in; 39.4 cm (Sotheby's)

CHIPARUS *The Starfish Dancer* cold-painted bronze and ivory, onyx base 19 in; 48.2 cm

CHIPARUS *Dancer with Slit Skirt* cold-painted bronze and ivory, onyx base 25 in; 63.5 cm (Sotheby's)

CHIPARUS *Antinea* cold-painted bronze and ivory, black and gold marble base 27 in; 68.6 cm

CHIPARUS *La Mystérieuse* cold-painted bronze and ivory,
brown onyx base 16 in; 40.5 cm

CHIPARUS *The Sunburst Dress* cold-painted bronze and ivory, brown onyx base 23 in; 58.6 cm

CHIPARUS *Les Amis de Toujours (Eternal Friends)* cold-
painted bronze and ivory, onyx base 25 in; 63.75 cm

CHIPARUS *Tanara* cold-painted bronze and ivory, onyx base
12.5 in; 31.75 cm

CHIPARUS *Danseuse Hongroise* cold-painted bronze and
ivory, brown onyx base 19 in; 48.2 cm

CHIPARUS *Pierrot and Girl with Feathered Hat* cold-painted
bronze and ivory, onyx base 19.25 in; 49 cm (Sotheby's)

CHIPARUS *Pierrot and Colombine* silvered and cold-painted
bronze and ivory, tambour marble and mosaic base 14.1 in;
35.9 cm

CHIPARUS *Danseuse Hindoue* cold-painted bronze and ivory, marble base 15.4 in; 39 cm (Collection of Fulvia and Adolpho Leirner, Sao Paulo)

CHIPARUS *Ballets Russes* cold-painted bronze and ivory, marble base 21 in; 53.3 cm (Collection of Mr and Mrs Sydney Lewis, Richmond, Virginia)

CHIPARUS *Dancer with Lamp* cold-painted bronze and ivory,
onyx lamp 14.2 in; 36 cm (Collection of Fulvia and Adolpho
Leirner, Sao Paulo)

Opposite
DOROTHEA CHAROL *Dancer in Green* cold-painted bronze
and ivory, bronze and onyx base 15.75 in; 40 cm

CHIPARUS *The Echo* cold-painted bronze and ivory, marble
base 25.6 in; 60 cm (Collection of Fulvia and Adolpho
Leirner, Sao Paulo)

Opposite
F. PREISS *Con Brio* (Model No. 1140) cold-painted bronze
and ivory, banded green onyx and black marble base 14.5 in;
36.8 cm. The original price was 22 gns complete on a base,
24 gns on a tray

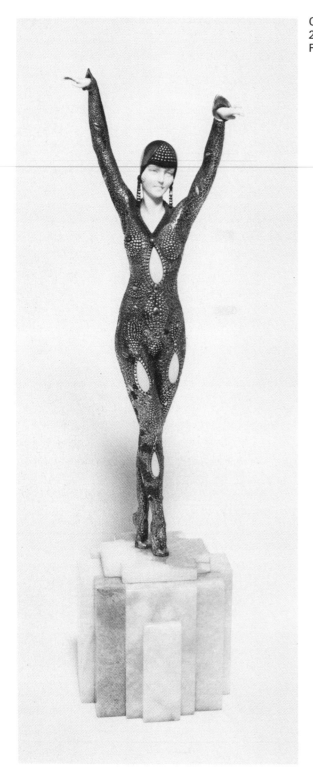

CHIPARUS *Dourga* cold-painted bronze and ivory, onyx base 24.75 in; 63 cm (Collection of Mr and Mrs Sydney Lewis, Richmond, Virginia)

PIERRE LE FAGUAYS *Dancer with Floral Skirt* cold-painted bronze and ivory, marble base 18.2 in; 46 cm (Collection of Fulvia and Adolpho Leirner, Sao Paulo)

PIERRE LE FAGUAYS *The Puppet Theatre* gilt bronze and ivory; rouge marble, alabaster and gilt bronze illuminated theatre 19 in; 48.2 cm

PIERRE LE FAGUAYS *Equestrienne* patinated bronze and ivory 14.2 in; 36 cm (Collection of Fulvia and Adolpho Leirner, Sao Paulo)

39

CARLO SARABEZOLLES *L'Ame de la France (The Soul of France)* 1922 bronze and ivory, marble base 15.7 in; 40 cm (Collection of Fulvia and Adolpho Leirner, Sao Paulo)

LEMO *The Circular Skirt* cold-painted bronze and ivory, onyx and alabaster base 13.8 in; 35 cm (Collection of Fulvia and Adolpho Leirner, Sao Paulo)

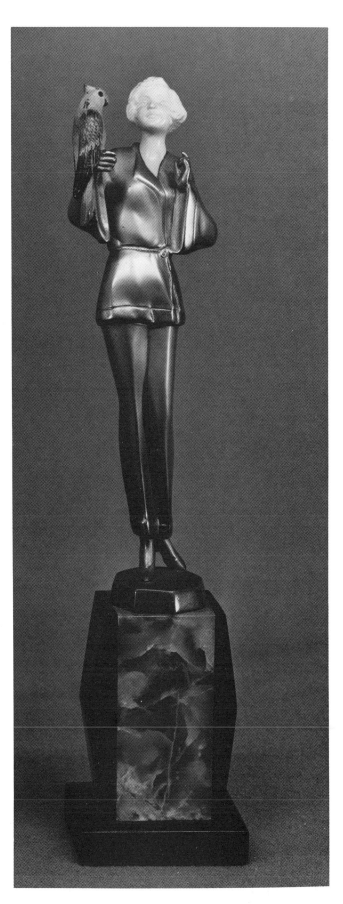

LORENZL *The Shawl* cold-painted bronze and ivory, green onyx base 9.6 in; 24.4 cm

LORENZL *Pajama Girl with Parrot* cold-painted bronze and ivory, green onyx and black marble base 12.5 in; 31.75 cm

LORENZL *Dancer* gilt bronze and ivory, green onyx base 9.3 in; 23.75 cm

LORENZL *Amazon* cold-painted bronze and ivory, green onyx base 9.1 in; 23.1 cm

PHILIPPE *Turkish Dancer with Parrot* cold-painted bronze and ivory, verde marble base 26 in; 66 cm

A. KELETY *The Shy Girl* cold-painted bronze and ivory, brown onyx base 13.8 in; 35.2 cm

PHILIPPE *Dancer with Turban* cold-painted bronze and ivory, green onyx base 26.25 in; 66.75 cm

Opposite
GERDAGO *Futuristic Dancer* cold-painted bronze and ivory, green onyx base 11 in; 27.9 cm

PHILIPPE *Dancer* cold-painted bronze and ivory, onyx base; other versions have a carved walnut body 21.5 in; 54.5 cm

44

Left: PIERRE LE FAGUAYS *Dancer* gilt bronze and ivory, green onyx base 11 in; 27.9 cm

Centre: F. PREISS *The Tambourine Dancer* cold-painted bronze and ivory, green onyx base 12.5 in; 31.8 cm

Right: LORENZL *Tambourine Dancer* cold-painted bronze and ivory; onyx tambourine; green onyx and black marble base 10.5 in; 26.7 cm

Opposite

PHILIPPE *Fan Dancer* cold-painted bronze and ivory, green onyx tray base 18 in; 46 cm

PHILIPPE *The Swirling Dress* cold-painted bronze and ivory,
green onyx base 15.75 in; 40 cm

Opposite
CHIPARUS *Dancer* cold-painted bronze and ivory, brown
onyx base 20.75 in; 52.7 cm

GODARD *The Bubble Dancer* cold-painted bronze and ivory,
glass bubble, black and gold marble and onyx base 20.75 in;
52.7 cm

GODARD *Turkish Dancer* cold-painted bronze and ivory, black and gold marble base 19.5 in; 50.5 cm

Odeon Dancer gilt bronze and ivory, onyx base 18.25 in;
46.4 cm

COLINET *Danseuse Hindoue* cold-painted bronze and ivory, bronze and onyx base 17.75 in; 45.1 cm

FUGÈRE *Salome* cold-painted bronze and ivory, green onyx base 17 in; 43.2 cm

53

COLINET *Danseuse D'Ankara* cold-painted bronze and ivory,
ochre marble base 24.1 in; 61.25 cm

COLINET *Danseuse de Thèbes* cold-painted bronze and ivory,
marble base with inset bronze plaque 10.6 in; 27 cm
(Collection of Fulvia and Adolpho Leirner, Sao Paulo)

COLINET *Small Exotic Dancer* cold-painted bronze and ivory,
onyx base 13.75 in; 34.9 cm

Opposite

PROF. O. POERZL *Medieval Lady with Two Hounds* cold-
painted bronze and ivory, green onyx base 16 in; 40.6 cm
(J. Martins and B. Forrest, London)

ROLAND PARIS *The Winged Dancer* cold-painted bronze and ivory, marble base 8.75 in; 22.25 cm (Collection of Mr and Mrs Sydney Lewis, Richmond, Virginia)

Opposite
CHIPARUS *Thaïs* cold-painted bronze and ivory, brown onyx base 20 in; 50.8 cm (J. Martins and B. Forrest, London)

ROLAND PARIS *The Rejected Suitor* cold-painted bronze and ivory, marble base 5.75 in; 14.75 cm (Collection of Fulvia and Adolpho Leirner, Sao Paolo)

59

ROLAND PARIS *Invocation to the Sun* matching pair, of
cold-painted bronze and ivory, onyx bases
Centre: ONIS *Throwing the Ball* gilt bronze and ivory, onyx
base 9 in; 22.9 cm

ALONZO *Apache Boy* gilt bronze and ivory, bronze base
7.1 in; 18.1 cm

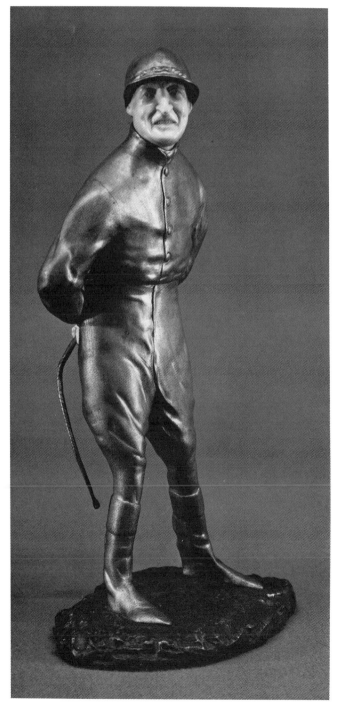

P. E. GOUREAY *Max Dearly as a Jockey* gilt bronze and
ivory, bronze base 14 in; 35.5 cm. Max Dearly was a very
famous French music hall comedian and monologuist, and
starred in one of René Clair's films. He was a partner of
Mistinguett, and pioneered the use of visual gags

61

BOURAINE *Pelicans* patinated bronze and ivory, verde marble
base 10 in; 25.4 cm

LAUREL *Bacchanalian Dancer* gilt bronze and tinted ivory,
wood base with intarsia decoration 11 in; 28 cm

SOSSON *The Skier* patinated bronze and ivory, onyx base
14.9 in; 37.8 cm

GERDAGO *Dancer in Floral Dress* cold-painted bronze and
ivory; green onyx base 12 in; 30.5 cm

JOË DESCOMPS *Nude with Scarf and Roses* ivory, banded
onyx base 8.5 in; 21.6 cm

JOË DESCOMPS *Nude with Trailing Scarf* ivory, onyx base
9 in; 22.9 cm

65

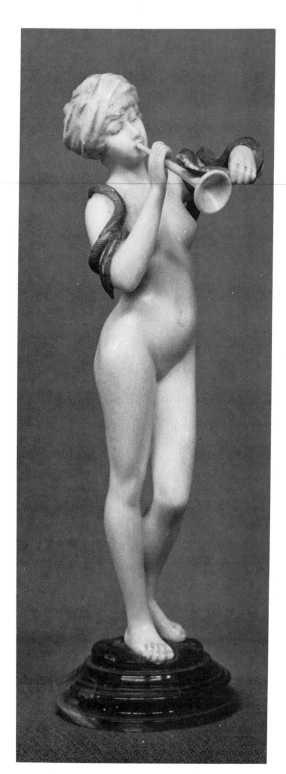

WIND *The Snake Charmer* cold-painted ivory; onyx base
7.25 in; 18.4 cm

KAESBACH *Nymph on Pedestal* tinted ivory, green onyx base
7.75 in; 19.7 cm

PROF. OTTO POERZEL *The Bat Dancer* cold-painted bronze inset with garnets, and ivory; green marble base   7.25 in; 18.4 cm

BRUNO ZACH *The Cigarette* patinated bronze and ivory, black marble base 26 in; 66 cm

BRUNO ZACH *The Black Leather Suit* patinated bronze and ivory, black marble base 25.25 in; 64 cm

68

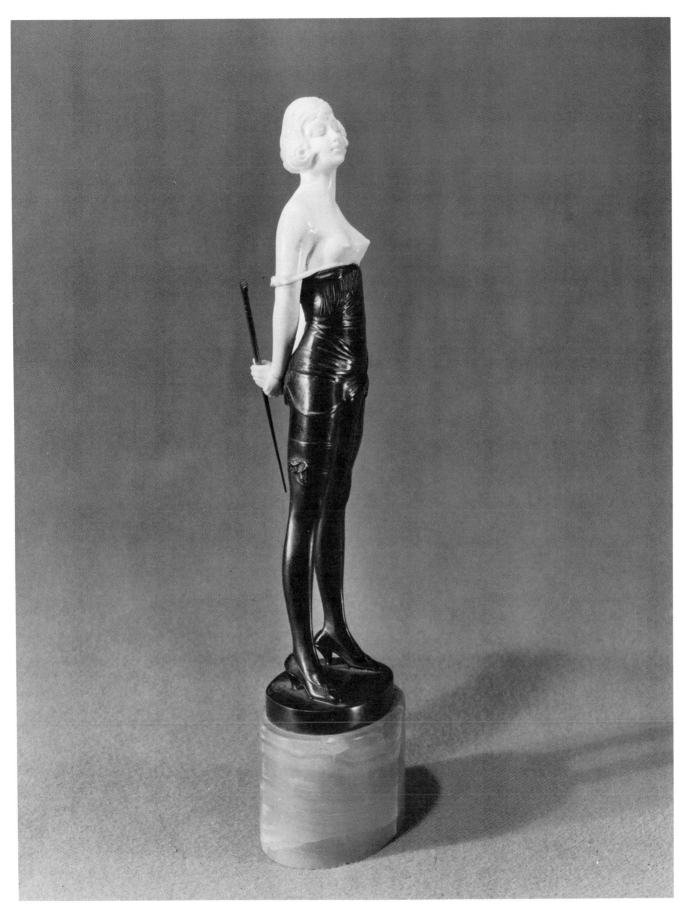

BRUNO ZACH *La Cravache (The Riding Crop)* patinated
bronze and ivory, black marble base 12.75 in; 32.4 cm

69

STENBERGER *Girl with a Ribbon in her Hair* gilt bronze and
ivory, rouge marble base 4 in; 10.2 cm

A. GILBERT *Pierrot with Guitar* gilt bronze and ivory, black
marble stepped base 11 in; 27.9 cm

F. PREISS *Aphrodite with Fruit Bowl* (Model No. 4529) and
Aphrodite (Model No. 2485) cold-painted bronze and ivory,
green onyx bases 10 in; 25.4 cm

F. PREISS *The Boy Skier* cold-painted bronze and ivory
10 in; 25.4 cm

F. PREISS *Aphrodite with hands clasped behind her head*
(Model No. 2485) cold-painted bronze and ivory, bronze base
fitted as lamp 10.1 in; 25.7 cm

F. PREISS *The Boy Angler* cold-painted bronze and ivory, green onyx base 12 in; 30.5 cm

Opposite
CHIPARUS *Dancer with Scarab Halter* cold-painted bronze and ivory, beige onyx base 21 in; 53.3 cm

F. PREISS *The Girl feeding a Pigeon* (Model No. 1139) ivory, green onyx base 7.25 in; 18.4 cm

Opposite

CHIPARUS *Snake Dancer* cold-painted bronze and ivory, onyx base 22 in; 55.9 cm

F. PREISS *The Bow Boy* (Model No. 1127) ivory, green onyx base 7 in; 17.8 cm

77

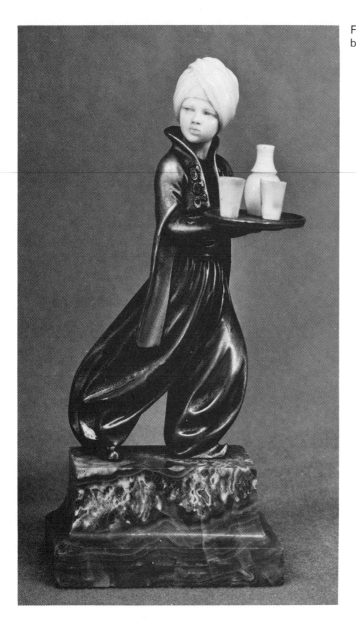

F. PREISS *The Turkish Boy* (Model No. 1135) cold-painted bronze and ivory, green onyx base 7 in; 17.8 cm

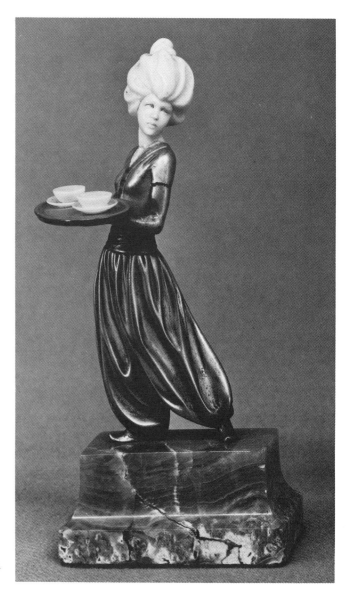

F. PREISS *The Turkish Girl* cold-painted bronze and ivory, green onyx base 7 in; 17.8 cm

F. PREISS *The Tune* ivory on green onyx base 6.4 in; 16.2 cm
The original price was 6 gns

F. PREISS *The Dancer* ivory on green onyx base 7 in;
17.8 cm

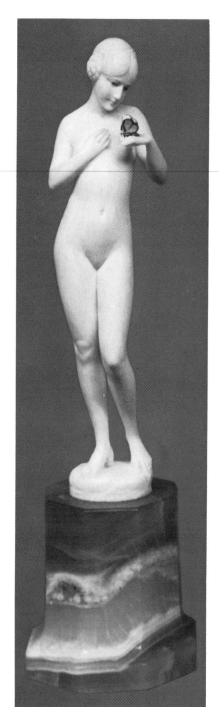

F. PREISS *The Butterfly* ivory on green onyx base 7 in;
17.8 cm

F. PREISS *The Parting* ivory on green onyx base 7 in;
17.8 cm

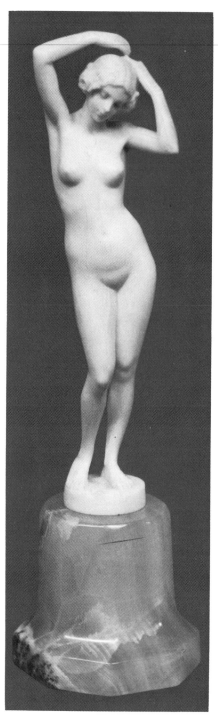

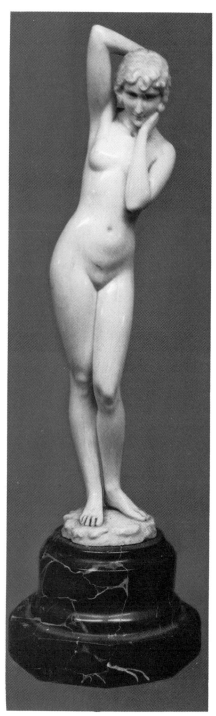

F. PREISS *Posing* ivory on black marble base 7.9 in;
20 cm

F. PREISS *Ecstasy* (Model No. 1130) ivory on black marble base 8.75 in; 21 cm (Collection of Mr and Mrs Sydney Lewis, Richmond, Virginia)

F. PREISS *Nude Dancing* (Model No. 1167) ivory on green onyx base 8.5 in; 21.6 cm

F. PREISS *Coyness* ivory on banded onyx and black marble base 9 in; 22.9 cm

F. PREISS *The Spring* ivory and marble 6.6 in; 16.8 cm

F. PREISS *Dancer* cold-painted bronze and ivory, marble base 9 in; 23 cm (Collection of Fulvia and Adolpho Leirner, Sao Paulo)

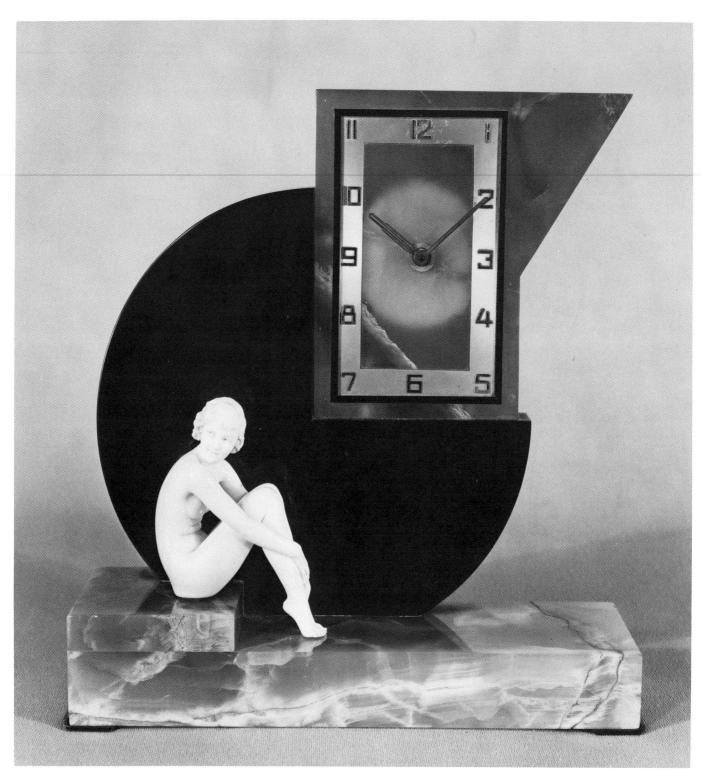

F. PREISS *The Clock* ivory, green onyx and black marble
10.3 in; 26.4 cm

F. PREISS *The Fashionable Girl* cold-painted bronze and
ivory, green onyx and black marble base 14.5 in; 36.8 cm

F. PREISS *Bather on Geometric Mound* cold-painted bronze and ivory, banded green onyx and black marble base 6 in; 13.2 cm

F. PREISS *Bather on Rock* cold-painted bronze and ivory on rough black marble base 10 in; 25.4 cm (Collection of Mr and Mrs Sydney Lewis, Richmond, Virginia)

F. PREISS *Salome Dancing* cold-painted bronze and ivory, banded green onyx and black marble base 13.5 in; 34.29 cm

F. PREISS *The Swirling Dress* cold-painted bronze and ivory, rouge marble base 7.5 in; 19 cm

F. PREISS *The Bat Dancer* (Model No. 1110) cold-painted
bronze and ivory, stepped green onyx base 9 in; 23 cm. This
was available on a base or tray and as a clock

F. PREIS *The Torch Dancer* (Model No. 1084) cold-painted bronze and ivory, green onyx base, composition flames 12.75 in; 32.4 cm. This was available on a base or tray, and in all bronze; there was also a version in sterling silver

F. PREISS *The Hoop Dancer* (Model No. 1164) cold-painted bronze and ivory, onyx base

F. PREISS *The Twins* (Model No. 1101) cold-painted bronze and ivory, onyx base

F. PREISS *Balancing* (Model No. 1126) cold-painted bronze and ivory, onyx base 15 in; 38 cm. The original price was 23 gns

F. PREISS *Dancer* (Model No. 1122) cold-painted bronze and ivory, onyx base

F. PREISS *The Beach Ball* (Model No. 1157) cold-painted bronze and ivory, onyx base

F. PREISS *Bowl with Caryatids* (Model No. 3355) cold-painted bronze and ivory, onyx bowl 5.75 in; 14.6 cm. The original price was 44 gns

F. PREISS *Carnival Couple* (Model No. 1124) cold-painted bronze and ivory, marble base

F. PREISS *Mandolin Player* (Model No. 1154) cold-painted bronze and ivory, onyx and marble base

F. PREISS *Charleston Dancer* (Model No. 1113) cold-painted bronze and ivory, marble base

F. PREISS *Medieval Lady with Two Hounds*
(Model No. 1158) cold-painted bronze and ivory,
onyx base

F. PREISS *Dancer* (Model No. 1119) cold-painted bronze
and ivory, onyx base 13.4 in; 34 cm. The original price was
16 gns

F. PREISS *Modern Dancer* (Model No. 1118) cold-painted
bronze and ivory, onyx base

F. PREISS *The Shawl* cold-painted bronze and ivory, green
onyx base

F. PREISS *The Champagne Dancer* cold-painted bronze and
ivory, brown onyx and black marble base 16.25 in; 41.3 cm

F. PREISS *The Flute Player* cold-painted bronze and ivory,
banded green onyx and black marble base   18 in; 45.75 cm
The original price was 28 gns

F. PREISS *Thoughts* ivory on black marble base
6 in; 15.2 cm

F. PREISS *The Tennis Player* cold-painted bronze
and ivory, green onyx base with ivory inserts 10 in;
25.4 cm

F. PREISS *Breasting the Tape* cold-painted bronze and ivory, green onyx base 10.5 in; 26.6 cm (Collection of Mr and Mrs Sydney Lewis, Richmond, Virginia)

F. PREISS *The Archer* cold-painted bronze and ivory, black marble base. This model was available in the sizes 10.25 in and 18 in, and in an all bronze version

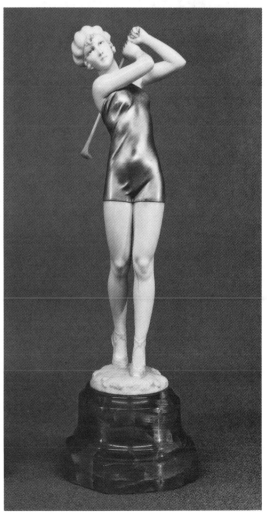

F. PREISS *Golfer in Bathing Suit* cold-painted bronze and ivory, green onyx base 13.5 in; 24 cm

F. PREISS *Bather with Parasol* cold-painted bronze and ivory,
black and gold marble base 9.9 in; 25 cm

F. PREISS *The Amazon* cold-painted bronze and ivory, green onyx and black marble base 17.25 in; 43.8 cm

F. PREISS *The Javelin Thrower* cold-painted bronze and
ivory, banded green onyx and black marble base   12.25 in;
31.1 cm

F. PREISS *The Golfer* cold-painted bronze and ivory, banded black marble and green onyx base 12 in; 30.5 cm

F. PREISS *The Culotte Dress* cold-painted bronze and ivory, onyx base 12 in; 30.5 cm

F. PREISS *The Ice Skater* cold-painted bronze and ivory,
banded green onyx and black marble base 13.25 in; 33.7 cm

F. PREISS *Brigitte Helm in Metropolis* cold-painted bronze
and ivory, stepped black and gold marble base 21 in; 53.3 cm

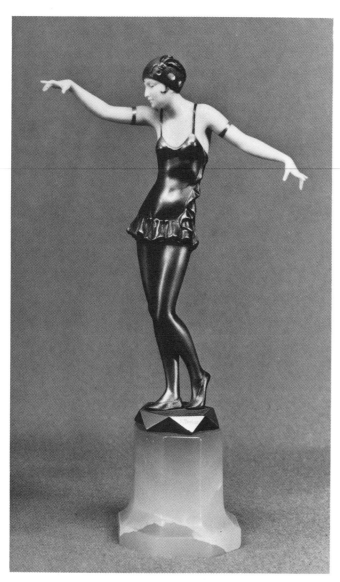

F. PREISS *Dancer with Feathered Toque* cold-painted bronze and ivory, green onyx base 9.5 in; 24.1 cm

PHILIPPE *Andalusian Dancer* cold-painted bronze and ivory; bronze and black marble base 14 in; 35.6 cm

F. PREISS *The Bee* ivory on onyx base 6.75 in; 17.1 cm

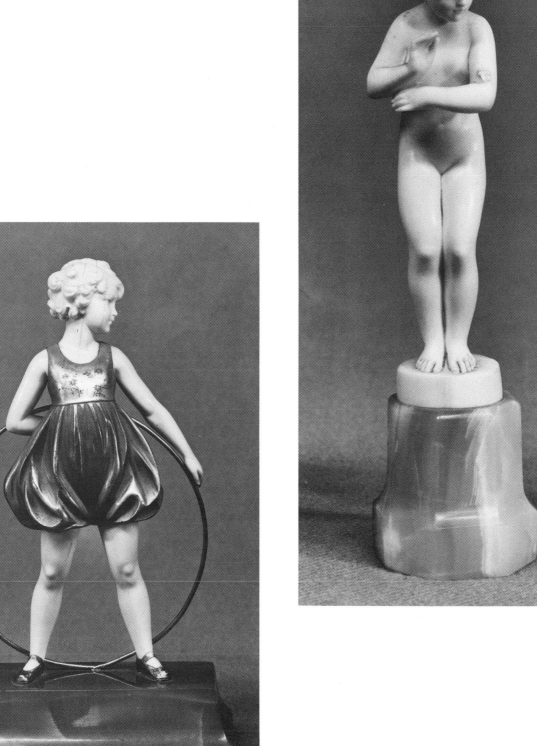

F. PREISS *The Hoop Girl* cold-painted bronze and ivory, green onyx base 7.75 in; 19.7 cm. The original price was 14 gns

PHILIPPE *Le Grand Ecart Respectueux (The Respectful Splits)*
cold-painted bronze and ivory, black marble base 7 in; 17.9 cm

Harlequin Dancer green patinated bronze and ivory, green
onyx tray 11 in; 28 cm (Collection Joan Collins and Ron
Kass, London)